# WELCOME

Hi!

As you read this, is your device within arm's reach, if not closer?

Don't worry if your answer is yes. Adults do it too.

It's a reality we all share—our phones have become the seekers of our attention.

They're our lifelines connecting us with family, they keep us linked to our friends, and they let us know whatever else may be happening online...even if we don't really care. They grab us and hook us.

That's intentional.

Think of the last time you went a day without your phone. Almost impossible to do? That's normal, one, two, three days cold turkey will be nearly impossible. (Don't worry, I'm not here to make you get rid of it.)

In the chaos of your daily physical responsibilities (school, clubs, friendships, sports, home life, etc), stress can increase even more with the simple tap of a "like", the flick of a scroll, or the sound of a notification.

It's vital to learn about what's happening with your attention, and develop healthier habits to navigate your device and online life.

# contents

# INTRODUCTION

"Almost everything will work again if you unplug it for
a few minutes, including you."
— Anne Lamott

# What You'll Find Inside

**Why Digital Wellness Matters –**
How screen time affects your mental and physical health, plus ways to take control of your digital habits.

**Navigating Online Challenges –**
From social media pressures to screen time struggles, get practical tips for handling common digital dilemmas.

**Building Healthier Tech Habits –**
Learn strategies to create balance, set boundaries, and use tech in a way that supports you.

**START HERE**

Let's be real—our phones are basically part of our lives. We use them for everything: texting, gaming, scrolling, snapping, and sometimes even learning. But have you ever felt like your phone is using you more than you're using it?

 Maybe you've caught yourself mindlessly scrolling, losing hours without even realizing it. Or maybe your phone is the reason for arguments at home—because ugh, parents just don't get it, right?

The truth is, being online isn't bad—but getting lost in it? That's when things get messy. That's where balance comes in.

"The price of anything is the amount of life you exchange for it."
–Henry David Thoreau

*What are we missing or giving up during the time we're online?*

This guide isn't about forcing you to give up your phone or deleting every app you love. It's about helping you use your devices smarter—so they work for you instead of draining your time, energy, and focus. It's about:

- Learning to set boundaries that actually make your life better

- Recognizing when your screen habits might be affecting your mood or relationships

- Finding ways to stay connected without feeling stuck in a digital loop

Just like eating junk food all the time can make you feel sluggish, mindless tech use can mess with your mental and emotional well-being.

But when you start using your phone with purpose, you get to control your digital world instead of letting it control you.

This guide is here to help you figure out what works for you—without lectures, guilt trips, or unrealistic rules.

Ready to take back your time and make your digital life work for you?

Let's go.

# WAIT... LIFE STILL HAPPENS WITHOUT MY PHONE?

If this workbook landed in your hands, chances are a parent, teacher, or counselor thought it might help.

Maybe they've noticed that screen time is messing with your mood or stress levels. Maybe they just want you to think about your habits.

Here's the thing: **Taking breaks from your phone doesn't mean missing out**. In fact, a lot of teens say they feel relieved when they unplug—less stress, better focus, and fewer arguments at home.

Often you hear, "Teens don't want to listen to adults!" when the truth is, you probably just don't want someone telling you what to do.

That's why this workbook is different. **It's not about rules—it's about you**. It's packed with quick reflection prompts and activities to help you:

✔ Figure out what's actually draining your time and energy

✔ Set digital boundaries that make sense for your life

✔ Stress less and feel more in control of your screen habits

You can navigate the digital world in a way that works for you—and yeah, even with some help from the adults in your life.

# WHY DIGITAL WELLNESS MATTERS

Tech is a huge part of your daily life—just like it is for the adults around you.

The difference?

You communicate in snaps, texts, emojis, and quick replies, while they think in full sentences and emails.

It used to drive me crazy as a parent… but I get it now! Those "one-word" conversations? They're real connections, and they do matter.

But just like in real life, balance is key.

Digital wellness isn't about detoxing, banning, or blocking—it's about you taking control of your online habits in a way that supports your mental and emotional health.

That's where this workbook comes in.

It's packed with tools to help you reflect on your screen use and create healthier digital habits—without giving up what you love.

# 1

## COMMON CONCERNS FOR TWEENS AND TEENS

Before you reach for your phone, take a second to ask yourself—why am I picking this up? Am I bored? Lonely? Procrastinating? Sometimes, scrolling helps in the short term but can actually makes us feel worse in the long run. Instead, try making a list of go-to activities for when you need a break—like stepping outside, doodling, listening to music, baking, or texting a friend.

# Tweens and Teens

A lot happens when you become a tween.

School gets harder, friendships shift, your body changes, and your brain matures. You start craving more independence, friends become a bigger part of your world, and social acceptance feels more important than ever.

And then, there's the first phone request.

That's when things get even more complicated—navigating rules, setting expectations, and understanding how to keep your mental health in check while being online. It's a lot!

But here's the good news: this is the perfect time to sit down with your parents or guardians and create a plan together.

Then comes the teen years.

Friends become everything. They're your go-to for advice, problems, and just about everything in between. You're out more, figuring out your identity, juggling school, and handling bigger responsibilities.

Even if you've had a phone for years, mistakes will still happen. That's normal. What matters is knowing how to learn from them and having the right tools to find balance, set boundaries, and protect your mental health online.

Digital wellness isn't about restrictions—it's about helping you build healthy habits now that will stick with you for life.

HEATHER BARNARD                    @TECHHEALTHYFAMILIES

# Signs of Digital Overload

Spending time online is fun, but too much screen time can take a toll—sometimes in ways you don't even realize. Here are some signs that you might need a digital reset:

**Trouble Sleeping** – Struggling to fall asleep or waking up feeling exhausted? Screens before bed could be why.

**Slipping Grades** – If focusing on schoolwork feels harder, constant screen time might be affecting your concentration.

**Pulling Away from Friends & Family** – Are you avoiding in-person interactions? Social withdrawal is a big sign of imbalance.

**Irritability & Mood Swings** – Feeling extra annoyed or overwhelmed? Your online habits could be playing a role.

**Less Physical Activity** – Sitting all day? Your body and brain need movement to stay healthy.

**Shorter Attention Span** – Finding it harder to focus? Constant notifications and endless scrolling might be training your brain to jump from one thing to the next.

**Body Aches & Pains** – Sore eyes, headaches, neck, back or hand pain? These are signs your body is telling you to take a break.

# Listen to Your Body & Mind

Taking breaks matters!

Even small changes—like standing up every 20 minutes, stretching, or going outside—can help.

Your body and mind will tell you when something feels off. The question is: are you listening?

Take a second to think—how many of these signs have you felt?

Have you been ignoring them?

It's never too late to make some small changes for a better balance.

HEATHER BARNARD                    @TECHHEALTHYFAMILIES

# Let's Get Real About Your Screen Time

Before we dive into this journey, take a moment to be honest with yourself about your relationship with technology. This isn't about judgment—it's about awareness. Understanding your screen habits now will help you figure out what's working and what might need a little adjusting.

How much time do you actually spend on devices? Think about your entire day. How many hours do you spend on screens? Be specific—what apps, games, or activities take up most of your time?

How often do your devices pull your attention away? Do you find yourself checking your phone when you should be focusing on something else? What usually distracts you (notifications, messages, boredom)? And how do you feel when it happens?

Have you ever felt like you're on your screen too much? If so, what did you do about it—if anything? Did you just push the thought away, or have you tried setting limits for yourself?

Is your device always on your mind? Do you catch yourself thinking about what you're missing while you're offline?

Are you using screens to avoid or escape? Do you scroll or game to avoid homework, chores, talking to people, or dealing with stress or feelings?

Have you ever tried to cut back? Have you actually tried reducing your screen time? What did you do, and did it work? If not, why do you think that was?

How do you feel when you can't use your device? Do you get frustrated, restless, or even angry when you don't have access to your phone?

If you feel comfortable, it might be a good time to share your answers with your parents/guardian, and ask what they see in your behaviors when it comes to technology. There's nothing wrong with feedback to help you reflect.

# IS IT ADDICTION OR JUST A HOBBY? LET'S TALK ABOUT IT.

The word addiction gets thrown around a lot when it comes to screens.

"You're addicted to gaming."

"You're always on your phone."

Sound familiar?

But **what** you're doing online and **who** you're doing it with matter just as much as **how** much time you're spending on your device.

Are you actively engaging—talking, creating, learning—or just passively scrolling?

Are you ignoring responsibilities, skipping meals, or withdrawing from family and friends?

For example, my son is a gamer.

At first, I worried. But once I took the time to understand his world, I saw he was strategizing, socializing, and developing teamwork skills.

Now?

He's in college, thriving, and gaming is just a small way he keeps in touch with friends.

## The key?

Balance.

It's easy to misjudge. That's why it's important to check in with yourself regularly and recognize the signs of overload.

**Technology should add to your life, not take away from it.**

**Take a moment**: How does your screen time make you feel?

HEATHER BARNARD                    @TECHHEALTHYFAMILIES

# Starting Your Digital Journey: Learning the Ropes

**Getting your first phone or device is exciting**—it's a new level of freedom and connection! But like learning to ride a bike or walking to your friend's house alone for the first time, or swimming, you need guidance, practice, and support before you do it on your own.

Think of it this way:

Would your parents or guardians hand you a two-wheel bike and say, "Good luck!"? Or leave you on your own without directions to find your friend's house? Or leave you in the water unattended?

No way! They'd start by helping you practice, teaching you the rules, and making sure you're protected.

The same goes for your digital world. Get started by:

- Having real conversations about screen time, social media, and privacy
- Building healthy habits that will last
- Setting boundaries with your parents/guardians, it's not a free-for-all!

It's not about restrictions—it's about learning together and making sure technology helps, rather than hurts, your life.

So, what's one habit you can start working on today?

HEATHER BARNARD                    @TECHHEALTHYFAMILIES

# Proving You're Ready:
# 4 Steps to Digital Responsibility

Getting a phone or social media isn't just about having fun—it's about showing you can handle it responsibly. Want to prove you're ready? Start with these four steps:

### Set Up Accounts Together
Don't just click "agree" on everything! Sit down with your parent/guardian to check privacy settings, location permissions, and any risks that come with different apps. Not all platforms are the same!

### Create Tech-Free Homework Zones
Distractions make homework 10x harder! Work with your family to set up a tech-free study space so you can focus and get work done faster (then have more free time!).

### Take on Social Media When You're Ready
Social media isn't a race. Talk with your parent/guardian about when it makes sense for you. Ask questions, do research, and share your thoughts. And when you do start, keep the conversations going!

### Find Your Balance
Screens are fun, but so are real-life activities! What do YOU want to do off-screen? Sports? Music? Art? Make time for things that fuel your energy and creativity.

HEATHER BARNARD

@TECHHEALTHYFAMILIES

# Taking Ownership of Your Digital Life as a Teen

By the time you're a teen, you've likely had your phone for a while—maybe not. Either way, it's never too late to start thinking about digital wellness.

**The key?**

Opening the conversation—both with your parents/guardians and with yourself.

**Real talk from students:**

In my work with middle schoolers, two things always come up:

- They get frustrated by how some peers behave online—things like oversharing, drama, or reckless posting.

- They actually wish their parents were more involved—not to control them, but to listen and talk through things.

You don't have to figure it all out alone. How do you want your digital world to look? What would make it feel healthier, safer, and more balanced?

Starting these conversations—at home or with friends—is a sign of real digital responsibility.

HEATHER BARNARD                    @TECHHEALTHYFAMILIES

# Building Digital Responsibility: 4 Steps to Take Control

Taking ownership of your digital life isn't just about rules—it's about making smart choices that help you feel safe, balanced, and in control. Here are four steps to start:

**Handling Problems Online:**
You don't have to navigate tough situations alone. Talking to a trusted adult can help you think critically and feel supported when things get complicated.

**Privacy Settings Matter:**
Instead of just accepting default settings, work with your parents/guardian to create fair and protective privacy settings that make you comfortable with who sees your info.

**Family Device Agreements:**
Tech boundaries shouldn't be just for kids! Creating family-wide screen-free times—like at dinner— helps everyone be more present.

**Setting Boundaries for YOU:**
Your physical and mental health are connected to your online world. Are you choosing content that lifts you up? Are you taking breaks when needed? These choices are yours to make.

HEATHER BARNARD                          @TECHHEALTHYFAMILIES

# Reflection on Digital Responsibility

Time for a quick self-check-in! This activity is all about opening the conversation with your parent or guardian—without judgment. Ask them the following questions and really listen to their answers. It's a chance to reflect on where you are and where you might want to make changes.

Do you think I'm responsible with my device? Why or why not?

Do you think I manage my screen time well? Why or why not?

Do you feel we communicate well about screen time? Why or why not?

What would you like to see change?

# 2

## UNDERSTANDING DIGITAL WELLNESS

Have you ever picked up your phone for a 'quick check' and then suddenly 30 minutes have passed? That's not an accident—apps and platforms are designed to keep you scrolling. But knowing this means you can take small steps to take control of your screen time, rather than letting it control you.

# Digital Habits Check-In

Let's take a moment to reflect on your tech habits. There's no right or wrong—just an honest check-in with yourself.

Rate yourself on a scale of 1 to 5 (1 = Not at all, 5 = Most of the time) and jot down why you chose that number.

Do you lose focus on what you're doing due to **notifications** from your device?

Do you have trouble concentrating on what you're doing because of **FOMO***?

Do you feel **anxious** or **stressed** out while using your phone?

Do you **check your phone** the first minutes of waking up each morning? What about while talking to someone?

Do you feel drawn to checking your phone **multiple times an hour**? Why?

*FOMO: Fear of missing out*

---

HEATHER BARNARD                    @TECHHEALTHYFAMILIES

# Social Media Habits Check-In

Let's take a closer look at where you're spending your time online. This reflection isn't about quitting social media—it's about understanding your habits and whether they're working for you.

Which social media apps do you use daily or hourly?
(Checking these off can help you see where most of your time is going!)

☐ Snapchat                    ☐ WhatsApp

☐ Instagram                   ☐ YouTube

☐ Facebook                    ☐ TikTok

☐ Pinterest                   ☐ Other:

*If there's apps that you have, and don't use frequently, or at all, have you considered deleting them? Now would be a great time as we work on digital wellness.

Do you have multiple profiles on any platform?
If yes, which ones? (Juggling multiple accounts can sometimes add stress or pressure.)

☐ Snapchat                    ☐ WhatsApp

☐ Instagram                   ☐ YouTube

☐ Facebook                    ☐ TikTok

☐ Pinterest                   ☐ Other:

Are there any accounts you wish you could delete but feel like you can't? What's holding you back?

☐ Snapchat                    ☐ WhatsApp

☐ Instagram                   ☐ YouTube

☐ Facebook                    ☐ TikTok

☐ Pinterest                   ☐ Other:

☀️ **Morning**: Start your day without your phone. Instead, shower, eat breakfast, and connect with family. It's a simple way to ground yourself before diving into the digital world.

🌿 **Afternoon**: Give yourself unplugged time during lunch. Eat outside if you can, talk to friends, or just take a moment for yourself—you NEED time to decompress!

🌙 **Evening**: Take at least 30 minutes of screen-free time before bed. This helps your mind relax and improves sleep.

## What is Digital Wellness?

Digital wellness isn't about quitting tech—it's about using it in a way that works for you instead of letting it control you.

✅ It's about awareness—noticing how you feel when using tech.

✅ It's about intention—using tech for a reason, not just mindless scrolling.

✅ It's about balance—finding time for both the digital world and the real world.

You don't need to quit gaming or delete your favorite apps. Instead, small habit shifts can help you feel better, stay focused, and still enjoy tech.

**Emotions**
Be mindful of your emotions. Take notice of how you are feeling after using technology. If you often reach for your phone when feeling bored, lonely, or overwhelmed, try keeping a list of alternative activities to turn to instead!

# What is Digital Wellness?

Digital wellness covers many areas of life, but as a tween or teen, these four areas are the ones that can make the biggest impact on your daily well-being.

If you had to choose two areas to focus on right now, which would they be? And within those, which specific habits or skills could you start working on today?

## Physical

- ☐ Reducing screen time before bed for better sleep
- ☐ Taking breaks from screens to move your body
- ☐ Avoiding eye strain and poor posture

## Mental

- ☐ Recognizing when social media is making you feel worse
- ☐ Managing stress and anxiety related to being online
- ☐ Creating screen-free moments for mindfulness and self-care

## Relationships

- ☐ Setting boundaries for social media and messaging
- ☐ Being more present in face-to-face conversations
- ☐ Understanding how online interactions impact friendships

## Productivity

- ☐ Avoiding distractions while doing homework
- ☐ Limiting notifications that pull your attention away
- ☐ Creating a healthy balance between online and offline life

# Self-Reflection

On this page, write down the two topics you chose from the previous activity. In the box next to each one, think about the subtopics you ticked off.

**What support do you think you would need to get started?**
Think about what kind of help or resources would make it easier for you to begin working on these topics.

**Who could be someone to help keep you accountable?**
Having someone to check in with can make a big difference. Who would be a good person to help you stay on track with your goals?

Topic:

Support? What? Accountable? Who?

Topic:

Support? What? Accountable? Who?

# The Impact on Your Well-being... the Down Side

Let's get the negatives out of the way. You've probably heard them a lot, but they're important to consider.

I'm all for using tech in a positive way—when you have the right tools to manage it.

Instead of banning or blocking, I believe in modeling and monitoring. It's about reflecting on how we use tech and creating balance.

I don't say to ignore tech, but to understand it better and keep an open dialogue with your parents.

- Excessive screen time **CAN** lead to stress, anxiety, or even lack of motivation. It **CAN** mess with your sleep, behavior, and social skills. Social media **CAN** contribute to anxiety, depression, and low self-esteem. If it's a part of your life, it's important to learn how to navigate it healthily.

- Tech **CAN** also impact face-to-face communication. It's something I worry about too, especially when my kids are texting from the next room! It's not just about isolation, but also about keeping those empathy skills sharp.

**Digital Addiction:** We are very quick to throw around the term "addiction" when it comes to being on devices. This term is for a very serious dependency which interferes with daily life and relationships, and the person is often unaware. If you're concerned about being addicted, you might need help setting boundaries and building healthier habits around your tech use, or intervention. Best thing to do is to talk to someone you trust.

# The Down Side Thoughts

Take a moment to reflect on the potential downsides of tech and screen time. Each time we reflect, we understand our behaviors better and spot where changes might be needed.

Have you given up activities you used to enjoy? Which ones? Why?

_____

_____

_____

_____

_____

Do you ever feel anxious about your social media? Why?

_____

_____

_____

_____

_____

Have you developed poor texting habits, especially with parents or other adults?

_____

_____

_____

_____

_____

# The Impact on Your Well-being... the Up Side

This is my favorite part! While the negatives get a lot of attention, there's so much good that comes from tech. I became a digital wellness educator because I wanted to talk about the positives with YOU!

**Here's what I love:**

- **Access to learning** – From apps to AI and augmented reality, tech brings learning to life! It's easier than ever to access resources in and out of the classroom, even translating info into different languages.

- **Creativity & self-expression** – Platforms like TikTok let you explore and share hobbies, art, music, dance, and more. My hope is that you're using tech to learn, create, and express yourself in healthy ways.

- **Improved communication** – Tech helps families and friends stay connected anywhere, anytime. A quick video or text keeps relationships thriving!

## Did you know...

A study from the University of Oxford found that playing video games for less than an hour a day can actually improve mental health. Gamers reported feeling happier, more social, and healthier than those who didn't play.

The study found that individuals who played video games for <u>less than an hour per day</u> reported higher levels of happiness, social functioning, and overall mental health than those who did not play video games at all. This suggests that video games, when played in moderation, can be a fun and healthy way to unwind and improve one's wellbeing.

# The Up Side Thoughts

Take a moment to reflect on the positives of tech and screen time. Each reflection helps us understand our behaviors and see where changes might be needed.

What are your favorite learning apps, platforms, or tools? Why?

_____

_____

_____

_____

_____

How and where do you express yourself and share online? Do you feel supported?

_____

_____

_____

_____

_____

How has technology helped you stay connected and build relationships?

_____

_____

_____

_____

_____

# 3

## ESTABLISHING HEALTHY DIGITAL HABITS

One easy way to take a break is to make it just a little harder to get pulled back in. Try moving your most distracting apps to the second or third screen of your phone, turning off notifications and badges, or even switching your phone's display to grayscale— it's surprising how much less appealing it becomes!

# Tiny Habits

So far, we've covered common concerns about tech, explored your own habits, and highlighted the good that comes from tech.

**The key takeaway is BALANCE.**

I know, having talks about your tech use with your parents or guardians can sometimes lead to anger or frustration, but it doesn't have to anymore!

By reaching this point in the workbook, it shows you care about making positive changes.

If you approach these conversations with the goal of understanding each other, and use the tools in this section, you can start having meaningful, helpful talks.

The goal isn't for adults to block, criticize, or ban tech—it's usually driven by fear and a lack of understanding.

Instead, we want to provide tools that help create a healthier relationship with tech and work together with your parents or guardians to make it happen.

## Be Aware of Digital Hooks

Apps and platforms are designed to keep you online—autoplay, continuous scroll, notifications, and streaks all work to steal your attention. Since they won't help you set limits, you have to help yourself! Try turning off notifications, disabling autoplay, and putting time-consuming apps on the second or third screen of your phone.

# Tiny Habits Ideas

Tiny habits are simply processes we use to try and change a part of our lives for the better. We're trying to stop an unwanted behavior.

These are small habits you can start today to improve your mental health and create more balance in your life.

Start with just one tiny habit and focus on it for the next week (or even month).

Taking it slow helps you build a lasting habit—too many changes at once can backfire.

Use the next pages to track your progress and, more importantly, how you're feeling. Once you've made progress with one habit, come back and add another!

These are just a few ideas, but there are many more out there! Discuss them with your family and see what works for you.

Choose a tiny habit to start:

- ☐ Turn off notifications on apps
- ☐ Block specific times for social media use
- ☐ Have phone free dinners as family
- ☐ Keep phone out of bedroom at night
- ☐ Delete apps that aren't useful
- ☐ Take an eye break for every 20 minutes you're on a screen
- ☐ Use blue light filters or glasses
- ☐ Unfollow negative people
- ☐ Block tech-free (non-educational) times for homework/studying
- ☐ Eat lunch without your phone
- ☐ Eliminate tech 30 min before bed
- ☐ Reflect on mental state after social media use
- ☐ Get active for every hour of screen use (stretch, walk, play)
- ☐ Get an ergonomic set up
- ☐ Turn off "auto play" on platforms like Netflix, Hulu and YouTube

Now for the fun part! Let's work through your habit tracking to kickstart your digital wellness journey.

Remember, habits can take time to stick—sometimes up to 66 days! Start small, keep trying, and don't worry about taking away your tech—it's about finding balance.

**Step 1:** What habit did you choose from the list? How will you make it happen? Who can support you for accountability?

HABIT .................................................................................................

○

○

○

○

**Step 2:** Track your habit on the next page, and pay attention to how you feel during this time.

**Step 3:** Use the deeper reflection tool to see how these tiny habits can positively impact your life.

# Tiny Habits Tracker

Tracking your habits helps you stay on course and reach your goal. Mark off each day you successfully complete your habit. How many days or weeks did you manage? If you stumbled, no worries—just try again!

| | | | | |
|---|---|---|---|---|
| 1 | 2 | 3 | 4 | 5 |
| 6 | 7 | 8 | 9 | 10 |
| 11 | 12 | 13 | 14 | 15 |
| 16 | 17 | 18 | 19 | 20 |
| 21 | 22 | 23 | 24 | 25 |
| 26 | 27 | 28 | 29 | 30 |

REFLECTION NOTES

_____

_____

_____

_____

# Tiny Habits Tracker

Tracking your habits helps you stay on course and reach your goal. Mark off each day you successfully complete your habit. How many days or weeks did you manage? If you stumbled, no worries—just try again!

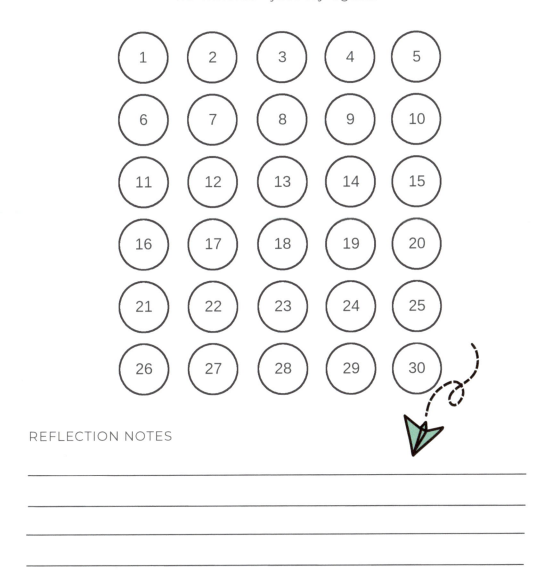

| 1 | 2 | 3 | 4 | 5 |
| 6 | 7 | 8 | 9 | 10 |
| 11 | 12 | 13 | 14 | 15 |
| 16 | 17 | 18 | 19 | 20 |
| 21 | 22 | 23 | 24 | 25 |
| 26 | 27 | 28 | 29 | 30 |

REFLECTION NOTES

_____

_____

_____

_____

# Tiny Habits Reflection

Take a moment to reflect on how sticking with your habit has impacted your physical and mental health, as well as your relationships.

Fill this out after keeping up with your habit for at least a couple of weeks. Repeat this reflection each time you try a new habit.

Be honest—there's no shame in recognizing that digital wellness can actually be pretty awesome! Get feedback from your family on how you're doing.

## Did you notice a difference?

| | No | A little | Often | Yes |
|---|---|---|---|---|
| I experienced less eye pain and strain | ○ | ○ | ○ | ○ |
| I had fewer headaches | ○ | ○ | ○ | ○ |
| I had less body aches (back, neck, wrist) | ○ | ○ | ○ | ○ |
| I slept better | ○ | ○ | ○ | ○ |
| I ate better meals and at better times | ○ | ○ | ○ | ○ |

## Did you notice a difference?

| | No | A little | Often | Yes |
|---|---|---|---|---|
| I felt less anxious | ○ | ○ | ○ | ○ |
| I had better connections with my family | ○ | ○ | ○ | ○ |
| I had better connections with my friends | ○ | ○ | ○ | ○ |
| I felt less stress | ○ | ○ | ○ | ○ |

# 4

## PROMOTING DIGITAL WELLNESS AND HEALTHY HABITS

Sometimes, small choices can add up. Before hitting play next on a video or diving into a long gaming session, ask yourself:
Will "future me" be glad I spent my time this way?
Is there something I'd rather do that I'll feel better about later?

Tech can be a great resource, especially when shared in a positive way, like creating something together or for someone else.

# Activities

## WITH TECH

- ☐ Have a video call with family
- ☐ Create a music playlist
- ☐ Take selfies together & enjoy the laughter
- ☐ Learn a new skill or hobby together
- ☐ Explore an app together, why do you like it?
- ☐ Listen to a podcast together (we love this)
- ☐ Listen to favorite music and dance it out!
- ☐ Have movie night
- ☐ Go geocaching
- ☐ Choose something on Pinterest to try
- ☐ Learn a TikTok dance
- ☐ Play a video game

Here are some ideas for building a healthy relationship with technology as a family!

This can include anyone in your household—and even extend to friends—because the goal is connection and strengthening relationships with tech.

When everyone supports the same goal of positive physical and mental health, it's much easier to stick to healthy habits.

Remember, tech doesn't have to be the enemy—it's our habits with it that need attention.

Sometimes, it's nice to just decompress —away from the buzz of notifications and the pressure of being online. It's about finding peace and being present with family and friends.

# Activities

## WITHOUT TECH

### Physical activities for the week

- ☐ Go for a walk together
- ☐ Plan an activity together and do it!
- ☐ Have a board game night
- ☐ Do some yoga or meditation
- ☐ Create your family charter
- ☐ Make vision boards
- ☐ Bake something together
- ☐ Have a device free dinner out
- ☐ Build a fort...at any age!
- ☐ Do a family book club
- ☐ Teach each other a hobby or skill
- ☐ Menu plan together
- ☐ Create an indoor or outdoor garden

This isn't a detox (remember, I'm not a fan of that word).

It's about giving your brain a break and finding balance so tech doesn't take over your life.

If you're online a lot, stepping away can be tough. We need a little "friction" to help us pause.

Ask your family for support —whether it's setting reminders, time blocking, or simply giving you a tap on the shoulder and saying, "Hey, let's do something!"

# FAMILY CHARTER

This tool is one of the most popular ways to quickly get your family on the same page when it comes to tech use.

For each person in your family, take a moment to reflect on the categories below. Write down what you're doing well and areas where you could improve with tech, including TV, gaming systems, phones, and computers.

This is a great opportunity to have open, honest conversations as a family about your tech habits.

Once you've reflected, set a goal for each person. By doing this together, you'll support each other in creating healthier tech habits, and the more you talk about it, the easier it becomes.

| FAMILY MEMBERS | WHAT I'M DOING WELL | WHERE I NEED IMPROVEMENT | MY GOALS |
|---|---|---|---|
|  |  |  |  |
|  |  |  |  |
|  |  |  |  |
|  |  |  |  |
|  |  |  |  |

# FamilyPledge

- - - - - - - - - - - - - - - - - - - - - - - - -

## Respect people around you

When using devices, we'll be mindful of our surroundings and the people around us. This includes turning off notifications, silencing sounds, and putting devices away when someone is talking to us.

## Practice healthy habits

We'll work together as a family to create healthy device use habits, like unplugging before bedtime, setting aside device-free times (such as dinner or homework), being present during family activities, and taking breaks for our eyes and minds.

## Set limits

Setting phone-free spaces in our daily lives. This could be the dinner table, the bedroom, or even a designated quiet space for focus and creativity. Tech-free moments help us feel present, productive, and relaxed.

## Be present

It's important to be present during activities and conversations. We'll agree to spend specific times together as a family or with friends without devices—like during meals, while playing games, or watching shows together.

## Stick to the plan

We'll hold each other accountable to follow this pledge and our agreed-upon habits. If we slip up, we'll remind each other of our goals and support each other in making positive changes.

You can always add more details using the customizable family pledge builder on my website later.

# Mindfulness Tips

### Pause before checking devices

- Take **five deep breaths** before checking your phone or computer to help you transition mindfully between activities.

### Reflect on your social media use

- While using social media, **pause and think** about how the content you're viewing makes you feel. If it doesn't make you feel good, consider unfollowing or taking a break from that account.

### Wind down before bed

- Avoid looking at screens for at least 30 minutes before bed to **help your brain relax** and wind down.

### Take regular breaks

- **Set a timer** to take a 10-15 minute break every hour from your phone or computer. Stretch, walk around, talk to someone, or practice deep breathing.

### Set tech boundaries

- **Turn off** notifications, **delete** unnecessary apps, and set up tech-free zones to create space for other activities.

### Be kind online

- When communicating with others online, take a moment to consider how your words might be received, and practice kindness and **empathy**.

There are times when it's nice to decompress with your favorite apps—but be mindful of why you're reaching for your phone. **Are you avoiding a task? Feeling lonely? Bored?** While scrolling might feel good at first, it can sometimes make us feel worse afterward.

Instead of automatically picking up your phone, try to pause and ask yourself: What else could I do right now? Make a list of activities you enjoy (reading, drawing, going outside, listening to music) and keep it somewhere visible. The more you turn to these alternatives, the easier it will be to break the habit of mindless scrolling.

# Quick Tips

Print this out and keep it as a reminder of simple ways to promote your digital wellness!

## Take Breaks

Give your eyes and mind a break by stepping away from screens. Try taking a 5-10 minute break every 20-30 minutes. Stretch, walk, or do something physical to refresh.

## Balance

Find a balance between your online and offline activities. Spend quality time with friends and family and pursue hobbies that don't involve screens!

## Multitasking

Multitasking is a myth! We can't focus on two cognitive tasks at once. Focus on one task at a time and minimize distractions to boost productivity.

## Stay Organized

Digital clutter can cause stress. Organize your apps and files, and prioritize your tasks to reduce overwhelm and stay on top of things.

## Sleep

Blue light from screens can interfere with your sleep. Avoid screens for 30 minutes to 1 hour before bed, and establish a relaxing nighttime routine.

## Emotions

Be mindful of your emotions when using technology. Notice how certain platforms, people, or content make you feel. Unfollow or mute negative influences.

# Digital Laundry: Declutter Your Digital Space!

Digital laundry? Yep! Thinking of it as decluttering and cleaning up your space.

When was the last time you organized your digital life? Take a look at your Google Drive, phone screens, social media accounts, and email. Do they cause you stress or anxiety? Is there a way you could organize them a bit better to help you be more productive? Here are some quick ways to get started:

### Organize Using Folders, Tabs, and Color

- Create folders for easy access, and use color-coding to organize apps and files based on categories (e.g., work, personal, creative).

### Delete Old Files, Emails, Photos, and Profiles

- Clear out things that no longer serve you. Old documents, emails, and photos just take up space and create unnecessary mental clutter.

### Unfollow Accounts Not Adding Value

- Social media should be a place that uplifts you. Unfollow accounts that don't bring joy or positivity to your feed.

### Use Categories for Organization

- Sort your digital life into categories like Creative, Productive, Work, and Entertainment to keep everything in its proper place.

### Unsubscribe from Unnecessary Email Groups

- Free yourself from unwanted newsletters or promotional emails. Organize your inbox for easier management.

### Close Tabs and Windows When Not in Use

- Keep your browser uncluttered and focused by closing unnecessary tabs. A clean screen leads to a clearer mind!

# CONCLUSION

If you're avoiding homework, chores, or a creative project because scrolling seems easier, try the 5-minute rule—just start for five minutes. Most of the time, you'll keep going and feel great about it. If not, at least you got started!

# Recap of Key Points

Technology can be an amazing tool for learning and connecting with others, but it's essential to use it thoughtfully to ensure your safety and well-being online. By being proactive and keeping open, honest conversations with friends and family, you can navigate the digital world with confidence and resilience. It's not all bad!

Understanding the risks is crucial because technology has become such an integral part of our lives, and its effects can be significant, especially for tweens and teens. Like it or not, you are highly impressionable at this stage, and excessive tech use can lead to consequences like shorter attention spans, less physical activity, and social isolation.

However, the good news is that small, positive changes—what we call "tiny habits"—can lead to a healthier relationship with technology. These habits can make a big difference in your overall well-being, helping you perform better in school, manage your mental health, and connect more meaningfully with others. It's all about balance.

Technology has many benefits for tweens and teens, including easy access to educational resources, opportunities for creativity and self-expression, and ways to stay connected. It's important to encourage each other to use it in positive and productive ways, so you can enjoy the benefits without letting it take over your life.

# About
## ME

Hi! I'm Heather Barnard, and I'm here to help you make the most of technology without letting it take over your life.

As a Certified Digital Wellness Educator, I know that tech can be amazing – it connects us, helps us learn, and lets us express ourselves.

But I also know that too much screen time or getting caught up in the wrong things can leave us feeling drained, distracted, or disconnected.

I'm a mom of three teens, so I totally get how tricky it can be to find balance.

Through my work, I'm here to show you how small habits can make a huge difference in keeping tech from controlling your world.

Let's make technology work for you, not the other way around!

## DO YOU NEED MORE HELP?

www.techhealthyfamilies.com

# notes

# notes

# notes

# notes

# notes

# notes